This Light that Pushes Me

Stories of African
Peacebuilders

Enter this book with care. Turn the pages slowly. Watch and read with respect, the kind that asks you to look, and then look again. Hold the gaze of these eyes longer than normal, for they speak from deep, too often invisible and silent pools of compassion. Listen, as they have, from the ear of the heart and you will find what has long been understood and true from Quaker tradition – there is that of God in every person. And when we notice that divine spark we feel the hope that our broken family can find the way to restitch the fabric of our common humanity. Here are the faces of our beloved community. Prepare to receive their gift and hold it close.

John Paul Lederach
Professor of International Peacebuilding,
Kroc Institute, University of Notre Dame

First published in April 2014

Quaker Books
Friends House
173 Euston Road
London NW1 2BJ

Designed by Cox Design, Witney

Printed by Berforts Information Press, Oxford

ISBN 978-1-907123-66-5

Registered charity number 1127633

www.quaker.org.uk

Contents

Foreword

To agree to have dialogue is the beginning of a peaceful resolution. ~ Somali Proverb

This Light that Pushes Me: Stories of African Peacebuilders presents photographs and personal testimonies of 25 people, which together tell one story. All the people in this book are involved with Quaker peacework and many are Quakers themselves. While the stories highlight various forms of violence, from the direct violence of genocide and civil war to the often invisible violence of exclusion, marginalisation and exploitation, this is not the focus of these stories. Rather the focus is on how people transcend those painful experiences, transforming them through gradual processes of personal healing into strength and optimism for peace and healing.

Quakerism was introduced to Africa in the early 1900s following the establishment of the first mission station in Kenya in 1902. Since this period, Quakers have been associated with social development, particularly concentrating on education, vocational training and the provision of health services.

While peacework among Quakers in South Africa was well established in the 1980s, in other parts of Africa the focus on peacebuilding increased dramatically after the genocide that took place in Rwanda and Burundi in 1994, where there was an urgent need to bring about healing and reconciliation across the communities that had been at war with one another. Through partnerships with Quakers from around the world, African Quakers began to look at peacebuilding in earnest.

The Quaker response to conflicts in the African Great Lakes region and neighbouring countries rekindled the flame among the current generation of Quakers to retrace the 350-year history of Quaker peacemaking since the days of George Fox. Peacemaking is embedded in the faith and practice of Quakers, and in most cases it follows the old tradition of quiet diplomacy without much visibility. It is grassroots focused and dominant in areas with Quaker presence in East Africa, the Great Lakes region, the West and Southern Africa. For Quakers, peacemaking is not a profession; rather it is a calling and hence requires sacrifice in terms of resources and a personal commitment.

This book therefore provides an opportunity to journey with the select experiences of a people who have chosen to pursue nonviolence, forgiveness and reconciliation over revenge, bitterness and violence. They are an expression of living Quaker values in action and the summation of the light that pushes, with the potential to transform attitudes and behaviours towards violence-free and more peaceable communities.

For the sake of peace, hard decisions must be made. ~ Tanzanian Proverb

Hezron Masitsa, Clerk
Quaker Peace Network – Africa

Introduction

If you really knew me and you really knew yourself, you would not have done this.
~ A banner hanging at a genocide memorial site in Rwanda

In some wars, neighbours turn on neighbours. Families are torn apart. Violence is immediate and intimate and leaves a thick residue of suspicion and hurt that cakes everything as thoroughly as the red dust of a continent thirsting for rain. We hear stories of helpless victims or of brutal perpetrators. We hear stories of peace summits and political negotiations and UN mandates.

There is another story. It is hidden, human, complicated. Whether in the midst of genocide, civil war, election disputes, domestic violence, or social exclusion, the individuals in this book have seen and experienced the worst that human beings can do to one another. And yet they consistently reach out to their enemies, seek to bring conflicting sides together, help others to emerge from the blinding cloud of their emotional trauma – not in spite of what they have experienced, but because of it.

Having worked in Rwanda, alongside a number of the people in this book, I witnessed the ability to use one's pain as a source of strength and found it profoundly challenging. I would often ask myself, "If faced with the same test, would I be able to do what I am watching my colleagues do? Would I have the courage, the spiritual grounding, and the personal grace to see my enemies as humans capable of change, to put myself in the line of fire, to risk ridicule from those I love?" When the idea for a storytelling project sprang independently from British Quakers and African Quakers, this was the seed that inspired a project to discover what drives these quiet peacebuilders and to share their stories more widely.

This book tells the personal stories of individuals from nine countries in sub-Saharan Africa. They are Quakers themselves or involved in Quaker peacebuilding work, most of it local and grassroots in nature. Africa is home to the largest number of Quakers in the world, with well over 200,000 active members in 19 countries. This is two-and-a-half times as many as are found in North America, and more than eight times the number found in Europe and the Middle East.

A fundamental aspect of Quakerism is that the Divine is present in everyone. It is an inner light, a "knowing" that we all can access no matter what we have done or what we believe. This one simple idea cuts across the vast differences in worship style and theology within the Quaker family, from the Programmed or Evangelical traditions common in Africa to the practice of silent worship found in Britain. It has led Quakers to campaign for the abolition of transatlantic slavery, to smuggle children out of Nazi Germany, to lobby for prison reform and to advocate for the universal right to conscientious objection.

In Africa, it has led African Quakers to bring enemies together to sit, talk and listen, and to work across divisions to tackle root causes of violence. The peacebuilding approaches help people connect with themselves and their own inner solutions and capacity for reconciliation. They are based on the principle that if you provide opportunities for people in conflict to encounter one another as human beings, they can rediscover the good in themselves and in the "other" and become whole again.

Some stories are accompanied by words that look like lines of poetry. These are quotations translated into English. Some people spoke in English and their exact words are faithfully recorded, even when the grammar is imperfect. They are arranged in "intonation units" – a new line started with each pause or new breath the speaker takes. The intention is to enable the reader to hear the cadence of the speaker's voice and thus feel the impact of the words more directly. In all cases, except for one, these "poems" are the direct quotations of the individual pictured. In the case of Emmanuel Haraka, he was interviewed along with his friend Joel Songambele, and the poem is Joel's.

The process of collecting the stories was a collaborative one. Many people in the book interviewed one another using a common set of structured questions as a guide. To the extent that geographical distance allowed, the summarised versions were shared with each person and in some cases rewritten collaboratively – either to fill in more detail or to edit out sensitive information that might endanger or embarrass someone if made public.

Excerpting from lengthy, textured interviews to create a cohesive whole was difficult because invariably when a frame is drawn around one aspect of a narrative it can risk defining a person too superficially. Thus, each story is not intended to encapsulate a person, but rather emphasises an aspect of their journey from violence, to healing, to activism. Taken together, they tell a collective story that stretches beyond these individuals, to countless others for whom the drive to build peace comes from deep within.

Weaving throughout these stories is the belief that some-where within our imperfect selves, however hidden under layers of grief, loss, tragedy, hurt, and disillusion, there is something good, something wise, something knowing. And it is this Divine kernel that pushes us to keep struggling to fix our broken world; to transform hurt and grief and the human lust for vengeance into something new, into a commitment to peace no matter the cost. This book invites us to do what the peacebuilders in this book have been striving to do for a long time: listen – with simplicity – for the truth. And when we hear it, let us walk side by side right into the heart of hurt, the deep and frightening darkness, and look for light.

Laura Shipler Chico
January 2014

Notes from the Photographer

Growing up in the North of England exposed me to a lot of violence. I was hospitalised for a week at the age of 11. My father's only advice was to be "more brutal" than my aggressors. That's the way they did things. Over the years I had more trips to the hospital and I in turn injured other people.

Years later in Bangkok I became friendly with a group of Buddhists. One day a young soldier on leave violently threatened a female friend of mine and I reacted equally to his violence. I expected my Buddhist friends to see me as a brave hero but instead they reacted with sadness. They said they only saw two violent angry people. The only winner in the situation was hatred. Feeling ashamed I took a vow of non-aggression and it changed my life.

This project was especially meaningful because I understand the process we go through to change. As a team we wanted the eventual viewers of these photographs to look into the faces and see the real person looking back. Our hope is you will glimpse something of their hearts and minds and possibly recognise something of yourself. We wanted the photographs to introduce the person to you, the viewers, as another human with the same emotions as you and I.

The photography itself was extremely personal and in most cases the person being photographed had usually just shared their own first-hand emotional story. The images were taken with the two of us sitting knee to knee, so close we could hear each other breathing. The interview sessions were at times extremely emotional and most of us shed tears, yet it is important to say that there was also a lot of laughter.

In the months since the project I have spent many an hour looking at these faces on a large computer screen and I often find myself doing nothing but looking back at the person.

My suggestion is for you, the reader, to look at the faces for a considerable amount of time. It is important to hold eye contact with the person rather than the photograph. I believe that if you do so for long enough you should see parts of yourself looking back at you.

Nigel Downes
Photographer

Rising

Cécile Nyiramana RWANDA

During Rwanda's 1994 genocide approximately 800,000 Tutsis and moderate Hutus were killed in just 100 days. As the genocide ended hundreds of thousands of Hutus fled Rwanda in fear of revenge killings. There were many intermarried couples and mixed families at that time. Cécile was targeted by génocidaires and survived by hiding in a friend's house before travelling with her husband to a refugee camp. After returning to Rwanda, her husband was imprisoned, accused of crimes of genocide. Unable to bear how her community and family had been torn apart, Cécile used her identity as both a survivor and a prisoner's wife to convince women from both sides to meet.

When I had that idea to bring together the widow survivors from the genocide and the prisoners' wives, some of my church members told me, "No no no no no, this is a waste of time. You will never achieve it." And I said, "No, let me try." And I went to one community and I asked some prisoners' wives to come together because on one side, I am a prisoner's wife. Then I presented the idea. "Are you willing to sit with the widow survivors, to face the truth, and also to break the barriers? Because they are supposed to be your enemies but we need to do something to prepare the future for our children." The women were open with me and said, "How can we sit with those women? We know they don't like us and we do not like them. And also we are sure that they will not accept to sit with us because of what our husbands did." This was a long, long discussion and finally they said, "OK, let's try."

Then I called another meeting with the widow survivors because I have many common things with them, as someone who lost some family members during the genocide. "What if us mums can come together with those prisoners' wives who are responsible [for] families like us, sit together and face the truth and talk about the genocide, and talk about the possible forgiveness and reconciliation?" And they said, "No, you are kidding. This is not possible! Those women?! Those prisoners' wives! We can't sit with them." We keep praying, we keep talking and finally they said, "OK, we can try."

Over time, these women built a profound bond and demonstrated remarkable acts of reconciliation. For example, genocide widows (Tutsis) helped prisoners' wives prepare and deliver meals to their husbands (Hutus), men who had participated in the killing of their own husbands and children.

*Someone can't forgive
with a broken heart.
We need first to heal our wounds
Our deep wounds
Then
Start the work of peace and reconciliation.*

*Sometimes
When you are still living
   with your deep wounds
It is not easy to forgive
And without forgiving
It is not easy to love someone.
They need to heal
Then forgive
Then love.*

Jao Sie "Samuka" Parker LIBERIA

Samuka fled violence in his home country of Liberia only to find himself engulfed in civil war in Sierra Leone. One day, he was forced into a queue waiting for rebels to amputate his hands or feet. "I was the 14th person to be amputated that day and Abdul [my friend] was the 15th person right behind me. And as we drew closer and closer and closer to where the amputation was going on, everything I had in me was gone. The spirit was out of my body." All of a sudden, one of the rebels recognised Abdul:

"Are you not Abdul? And is this not your brother?" He called my name, but I was not even paying attention because all hope was gone. And he said, "I'm talking to you. Don't you know me?... Step out of the line, the two of you." It was just a miracle.

The rebel convinced his commander to spare Abdul and Samuka. The experience deeply shifted Samuka's perspective, challenging his notions of perpetrators and victims in war.

If there is one perpetrator of a war
That could look at somebody
from nowhere
And have sympathy
And say no –
You don't deserve to go through this

If he could change
I believe
every other person
could change.

Théoneste Bizimana RWANDA

I was 13 years old when the killings started... During the genocide people were targeted not because they had done anything wrong but because of who they were. So as the little boy... I didn't understand... to see people die without any reason. I had to flee my country. I stayed in a refugee camp for [two] years and that made me suffer a lot. So I always questioned myself, why did this happen? Why did people do this?

As he grew, Théoneste felt drawn to help others who had experienced the genocide as children, who hadn't even known what tribe they were a part of before the war had started. Now he is the coordinator of Healing and Rebuilding Our Communities, a trauma recovery programme that brings genocide survivors together with perpetrators of the genocide to listen to one another and begin the long process of healing. His approach is based on the idea that in every person there is something good and that while anyone can suffer trauma, we all have an inherent intuition about how to heal. Théoneste helps people connect with their own inner wisdom and share that with others, restoring damaged trust in the process.

I decided to change my pain into a different idea,
a power to heal,
to heal myself
and to help others to heal.

I think people who have experienced the violence,
I think they still have something in them
that can change this experience into a powerful tool
to change themselves
and change their communities.
So it's still possible.
Not everything is gone.

Stanford Jarvis SOUTH AFRICA

Stanford Jarvis was a teacher for over 20 years in South Africa and is now Project Leader for the Alternatives to Violence Project in the Quaker Peace Centre in Cape Town, South Africa. When asked about his own experience of violence, he talked about shifting away from using violence as a tool in the classroom:

The way we used to discipline children in the schools was by using the cane. We used to beat them into submission instead of using alternative forms of discipline... As soon as you beat a child, you can see that something changes. You are closing down the communication, the relationship between you...

When I decided to put down [the cane] and use love instead, use compassion instead, use peaceful means of dealing with children, it just opened up so many doors for me. It just lights up their eyes when they come into your class and they experience love and they experience compassion. Instead of... humiliation and abuse, they just come into your class and they want to be with you all the time, all the time.

Believe in yourself.
Go in your inner deep
in your inner self
and do what you know
is the right thing to do.

Fatu Samah SIERRA LEONE

Fatu was 14 or 15 when the rebels attacked one day in her area. Her mother quickly coloured her and her sister's faces with charcoal and dressed them to look like old women to make them less appealing to the soldiers. When the rebels reached their house her mother directed the girls to hide beneath the bed. They asked her parents, "Where are your children?" and her mother said that they had gone away. But Fatu heard her younger brother say, "They are hiding under the bed. Our mother told them to go there." They came and grabbed Fatu out, but her sister remained hidden. Fatu was raped by five men that day while her family witnessed.

Today, Fatu hopes to get a Masters in public health and is working in a reintegration programme, helping rebels like those who hurt her to rebuild their lives. "Now I am working for peace," she says, "and I want whosoever did such a thing, too, should be at peace."

Adrien Niyongabo BURUNDI

It was night when Adrien suddenly heard shouting and crying outside their home. Immediately, Adrien went outside since the previous days had been so tense. A few minutes later, a group of Tutsi soldiers appeared and told everyone to lie on the ground. None of them obeyed. Instead, the whole crowd ran away.

Thanks to God! The soldiers were still human. They did not shoot in the crowd! It was a very dark night. There was no moon, nor stars in the sky that night. As folks were afraid to return to their homes for fear of being caught and killed, they tried to find refuge in the hills surrounding Musaga.

While climbing toward the hills, Adrien heard a voice stopping him and immediately was aware of guns pointing at him. It was the height of Burundi's civil war and after initial confusion he realised he had been stopped by Hutu militia mistaking him for a Tutsi. The voice of a passerby came out of the darkness. "Why did you stop that man? He is a Hutu." Adrien was released and kept following the queue to the hills. For fear of being mistaken again, Adrien decided to spend the night in the bush. During that long night, Adrien recognised that he had been very close to death and that God had spared him.

"Life was given back to me," says Adrien. "From that time I said... I need just to live my life by helping others." Adrien is the founder of Healing and Rebuilding Our Communities, which brings together Hutu, Tutsi and Twa in Burundi for intensive trauma recovery and community reconciliation processes.

*Healing
is different
from fixing.*

*It is easy to fix things
but it takes time for healing.
Healing asks courage,
compassion,
endurance,
and also self-giving.
It is risky also,
so you need to understand
that things will not unfold the way you are expecting.
So you need to expect the best,
just try
try.*

Nokuthula Mbete SOUTH AFRICA

Nokuthula grew up in apartheid South Africa. At the age of 21 she was raped. At first she told no one about the rape, afraid of being blamed by her family. "I met Quakers in 2001 when I started volunteering at Quaker Peace Centre. This is when I shared my story... I realised that these people are not judging me. Instead they listened to my stories... When I looked at [the man who raped me] I realised that there is something good in him."

Nokuthula now works to help young women recover from domestic abuse and rape, to rebuild their self-esteem and their lives. "What I'd like the world to know is that I am a strong beautiful woman who is there to see women growing, empowering women to stand up for themselves to find their voice, to know their rights."

Revenge
Hatred
Is not a solution

Start loving yourself
Start forgetting
Yes it is not easy

You will remember

But start feeling good about yourself
Start affirming yourself
That you are a good person
No matter what.

Leon Mkangya Alenga DEMOCRATIC REPUBLIC OF CONGO

During the war, I had a sister... It happened that people hid in the bush, and there was a need to get something to eat. And it happened that my sister went back home to get something to eat at that time. At that time when she was trying to return back home to get something to eat, she met soldiers. And when she met soldiers, the soldiers asked her why do you return back to this village when everybody has already left? This means that you are our enemy and that means that we are going to punish you. And my sister was killed with a sword and dropped in a toilet hole. This event touched me and I was totally traumatised.

Leon fled the war in Congo in 1996. He travelled by foot with his family the long distance to Tanzania and stayed there for some time. Eventually, he convinced his parents to allow him to return to Eastern Congo. "My aim was to come back and contribute to make peace in my country." The return journey was dangerous – he faced threats from rebels and the army alike. Now he is a community facilitator, helping others explore alternatives to violence. "All days are not the same," he says. "There are days of joy. And there are days that are difficult. Whether the days are difficult or joyful, we have to cope with it and not resist it."

Hezron Masitsa KENYA

Hezron was born out of wedlock and was raised by his grandparents from the age of three months. He later learned that when his mother had discovered she was pregnant with him, she approached the father but that that man's father, Hezron's paternal grandfather, had chased her away.

The father to my supposed father took a spear and said "you will never step on this compound, you try and I will kill you". When I look back it's just a miracle that I was living because my grandfather was so harsh. My mother was forced to drop out of school. My mother would have had two options – to abort or to commit suicide. But how she managed, I don't know.

Hezron's mother married twice but was maltreated by her first husband after he married a second wife, and as the second wife in her second marriage she was subjected to humiliation and dispossessed of her home and property. Later in life, he came to see his own longing for a father and the maltreatment of his mother as symptoms of a deep cultural violence. He has dedicated his life to trying to build peace and advocating for women's rights.

Where I am weak someone else is strong

We have to go deep inside ourselves
And admit that it is hard

We have to be bold enough
to admit that we have weaknesses
and it is only when we do that
that we can start to think about
how can we change
how can we be better
instead of living with some heavy load.

Florence Ntakarutimana BURUNDI

When she was a teenager, Florence's family fled the crisis and went to live with her maternal aunt. Over time, conflict grew between the sisters, with the aunt consumed with jealousy over how well her brother-in-law provided for her sister and the children. Florence believes that in 1997 her Tutsi mother was poisoned by her own sister. One year later, her Hutu father was killed by Hutu rebels who suspected him of being a Tutsi sympathiser after he refused to give up a Tutsi woman to be killed. "Hutus, they killed my father when he was a Hutu. The Tutsis killed my mother when she was a Tutsi. I was really confused."

Florence was left an orphan at 19 or 20 years old to care for her younger brother and sisters. After years of living in bitterness Florence was given the space in a trauma healing workshop to talk about her losses and trauma. She now works to bring together Hutus and Tutsis for trauma recovery and reconciliation. "You may try to revenge. And when you start a war, when you start a fight, you may know how it will start but you can never know how it will end."

It's good to commit to life
Because life is good

When you are in such situation and you say
That's the end of the world.
I am done, that's the end
The life is no longer good

There is still life

I used to say
As long as I am breathing
There is still
Hope in front of me.

Turning Point

Peter Serete KENYA

When post-election violence erupted in Kenya in 2008, Peter, along with many others, was involved in the response, bringing the parties together for carefully facilitated processes of reconciliation. He was not always a peacebuilder, however. He admits to once being in a conflict with the mother of his child. When she was pregnant, "I could even beat her, I could even violate her." The birth of his child transformed him. Now he says, "There is good in everyone. There is that of God in every one of us. So it doesn't give me title to hurt somebody who is also a human like me."

Everyone has a story to tell.
Many people have been neglected.
No one wants to listen to the pain of these people.
And the more we neglect them,
the more we ignore them,
we never listen to their stories,
they remain in that violence,
they remain in that pain for a long time.
And then at the end of it
it erupts like a volcano.

Getry Agiza KENYA

Getry Agiza was raised in a polygamous family, and when her father died there was bitter conflict between herself and her stepbrothers. As she grew older, she formed an opinion about the effect of polygamy and family violence on Kenyan society.

From that polygamy, all the friends of my stepbrothers become my enemies, all the friends of my stepsisters become my enemies, and that builds a society in hatred, and that builds a community in hatred and that builds even the tribes. And so we end up having the whole nation in fire.

Her own turning point came during a conflict transformation workshop, where she was asked to sit across from a partner and study her face while her partner closed her eyes.

The face of the woman became my own. First the woman looked beautiful. Then she became a beast. I saw so much pain... I had two options, to run away or to smash it... So I went out and started crying. And as I cried I wanted to be alone and then there was another facilitator who came and... sat behind me and he said, "Getry, if you need somebody to talk to, I am here." And I took like two hours sitting there and he didn't go...

I found myself telling him everything, and the true confession is I was planning to kill my stepbrother. I had a gang of young men who were very active, and one was trying to be my boyfriend. And I accepted because I wanted [them] to kill my brother, not because I liked him... It was almost the final week of the plan on how we can carry out the thing.

From this workshop I realised I was a human being, I had so much sadness. I grew up a very quiet girl, that I didn't see space of talking. That made me think about life again and... [I] didn't see the reason of holding a grudge... because it was denying myself happiness. So I just told them, you know what, I don't think we need to go ahead with that plan. I'm not comfortable doing it. And they were disappointed. They didn't like me changing my mind.

Getry is coordinator of the Friends Church Peace Teams and was instrumental in mediating conflict and reducing levels of violence in Mount Elgon, Turbo division and other hotspot communities in the lead up to the March 2013 elections.

Abdul Kamara SIERRA LEONE

During Sierra Leone's civil war, Abdul was captured and tortured by police and then captured and tortured by rebels.

I remember an incident when one of the rebels who raped my sister got captured... My friends came to me and said, "Come, we've captured the rebel who raped your sister. Let's go and kill him." And my neighbours, my brothers, they were all rushing down to finish them. I went there myself. I could not do it. It was difficult for me to take someone's life. I saw the guy. He was lying down. I said to myself, "You know, I'm better than this."

Years later, Abdul founded the Quaker Peace Network – West Africa, focusing on reintegration of ex-combatants. It meant associating with those who had tortured him, finding jobs for them and trying to create hope for them.

*My mother was very very disappointed in me
seeing me doing this reintegration.
She said, "What are you doing?
These are the people who tortured you.
These are the people who raped your sister.
These are the people who burnt your house.
And you know them.
What are you doing?
You are a disgrace."*

*I found myself not knowing what to do
whether to continue with my conviction to build peace
or to do what my mother said.*

Thank God I did what my conviction asked me to do.

George Walumoli UGANDA

George Walumoli became a peacebuilder after witnessing and experiencing violence in Uganda at the political level, the social level and even within families. He works with orphans, widows and widowers in his own community. He facilitates Alternatives to Violence Project workshops throughout the region.

Sometimes when you hold
The bad feelings within you
It is you who punishes yourself
So it is better to give up
And make peace
For your future.

Sizeli Marcellin RWANDA

When Sizeli reached Year 6 in primary school, he was one of the brightest in his class. However, because he was a Tutsi he was not allowed to advance to secondary school. He approached a seminary school known for accepting everyone, but they rejected him because his parents were divorced. With only a primary school education he became a baker and slowly built a life. "Then when I became a big man, the genocide came. I now had a big family, a nice family, a wife with three children. I had many relatives... The genocide took them."

After the killing, he became involved in trying to stitch his ripped community back together.

During that time people who were in the country were just accusing the people [who had fled] the country of committing the crimes. So once someone is back from outside the country he could face violence or revenge because one could say it was "so and so" who did this, but it was wrong. So I started to help people, those people who were inside the country and those who had come back just to bring them together to mediate. I remember this one guy called Pierre Damien. People had said that he had wanted to kill people in the church right here. One guy called Munyawera had said that Pierre Damien had chased him out of the church. But what we finally discovered is that yes, he told him to walk out of the church because he knew that people were coming to kill him... So I mediated them and helped them see this good thing in this story. So they became friends. It is not just them only. It is many people...

Realising the need was greater than these individual cases, Sizeli and others started the Friends Peace House, first helping to mediate, then helping people manage their trauma, and ultimately helping to reintegrate génocidaires back into the community.

And when I reached the place where I fled to
I realised there were many people who had more
more
many more deep...
problems than mine.
There were people who had wounds,
there were people who had been raped,
there were people who had witnessed their family being slaughtered.

This is the time that I got this light
that pushed me
to start helping
these people who had more problems than me.

Pastor Sarah Kakobwa BURUNDI

I had my sister-in-law. I loved her so much. She died because of the war. At that time, the men were in danger... so they ran away... It was my first time to see a person who died because they killed her. They came to call me and I went to see the place where the woman had died... When I got there, she was no longer conscious. I spent two hours with that dead body. I was just waiting to see if some people would come and go to bury her. People came and we went to bury her. What I did, I went to comfort my brother and his children, and I told him, "That is the world." That thing touched my heart, and that is why I start now to be a peacemaker.

Pastor Sarah went on to build peace quietly within her community. A lot of men had died during the war, and she saw how the women were suffering. She asked herself how she could bring them together. She began by bringing widows of the church together across ethnic lines to provide a space to talk about what was in their hearts. Connected by their mutual poverty and their need for stronger networks to help when they were sick or in crisis, the women created a group where they meet often as a family, called "Rema Ntiwihebure", meaning "Have Hope, Don't Be Discouraged".

They said now we have to work hard so that we can get something so that we can go and visit our friends who are suffering more than others. At that time there were men who did not have houses to live in. And those women said now we have to help those men who don't have houses and we have to go and look for grass to help those men build houses. After that, people started now coming together and sharing what they have. Now we started to cultivate. Today we go here, tomorrow we go there, but between us, we go to cultivate their land. So they become now friends.

The fear people had of living together began to diminish, and people shared their problems with each other. Some Tutsis who were in the internally displaced camps began to feel safe enough to move back into the community. Pastor Sarah continues her work, combining trauma healing and reconciliation efforts with practical initiatives that help people access clean water, raise livestock and develop small businesses.

If you have a problem,
If you continue to think bad things
To your neighbour or your friend
You cannot have peace in your heart.

Wherever you are
You will always think bad things.
It seems that the one with the problem
It seems that he carries the weight.

Even when you see bad things
It is good to forgive.
If you don't forgive
You cannot see God.

Let us forgive one another
So that God can forgive us too.

David Bucura RWANDA

Pastor Bucura was a leader in the Friends Church at the time of the genocide and was forced to flee to a refugee camp in the Democratic Republic of Congo. He returned as soon as he could and began to mediate between ethnic groups within the church and then in the broader community. He helped to found the Friends Peace House, bringing together genocide perpetrators and survivors for intensive community reconciliation processes.

I was one of the leaders of the Friends church here in Rwanda... It is not easy to live [with] someone who is suspect[ed] of kill[ing] your relatives, or your mother or your husband or whatever. It was a difficult time for some people to worship together, even to sit together... How to lead people who are not able to worship together, who are not able to sit together, even to talk? But as leaders we had some workshops... we started with ourselves because we cannot offer what we do not have. We started with Friends Church leaders, talking, coming together, and sharing our experiences from what we saw, from what we heard. We shared. And after sharing with people who passed through genocide... we said, "What to do now?" We said we need to do peacebuilding. It was after that we started to talk peace in our church.

From this modest beginning, Pastor Bucura went on to help with the reintegration of genocide perpetrators into society, and trained judges in Gacaca courts in alternatives to violence. "Gacaca" means "on the grass" and these courts were a traditional justice mechanism revived to deal with some genocide crimes. Many of the judges reported afterwards that the training had shifted the way they made decisions, and the way they listened for the truth rather than relying on hearsay.

Immediately after the genocide, Pastor Bucura reached across ethnic divisions to take in and support several orphans, regardless of their identities, and two of those children now are active peacebuilders in their own right.

We lost people.
We lost people.
Even relatives.
Relatives.
Friends.
Relatives.
Many many many many.
It was worse here in Rwanda.
I chose to be a peacebuilder because of that.

Violence brings only
Hatred
Death
Conflict
Blessed are the peacemakers
I think
People want to be
Blessed.

Walking into Fire

Rose Imbega KENYA

*I was in a matatu one day travelling from Kakamega...
I heard a conversation from two youths. They were
talking to each other arranging how they could come
and attack one tribe in our place...*

Mama Rose listened closely to their conversation. Kenya
had recently experienced grave post-election violence
that had resulted in over one thousand deaths and the
displacement of hundreds of thousands. Ethnic tensions
were partly to blame. Mama Rose was one of a number of
Kenyan Quakers to attempt to improve relations. On this
late afternoon, she alighted from the crowded van at the
same time as the two young men.

*I told them, please, I have heard all of your conversation
but I would like us to sit and talk. Please don't go and
attack these people... You come tomorrow to my house
and we'll talk. And they accepted. And I could not sleep
because I was worried they might turn and come and
attack me...*

*Now, the morning waked. When I saw them I was very
happy. I prepared tea... then we started the discussion...
They said, "We don't want Kikuyus here because they
are terrorising people... And yet they bought land here,
it is we who sold them land and yet they are abusing us."*

*So I told them, "Please, you just name for me one of the
Kikuyus who is terrorising." So they told me the name.
Then I said, "Please. From today don't go and attack
them. Now you have told me I will go and talk to them
and we will see the solution."*

The youth brought more people who were planning
attacks, and Mama Rose mediated their grievances. In
the end, violence was averted and Mama Rose remains
an important force for peace in that area.

Emmanuel Christopher Haraka TANZANIA

When violence erupted between Christians and Muslims in Nguruka, a village near Emmanuel's home, he and his friend Joel Songambele were worried: "Society was divided into two blocks – Christian and Muslims", Joel remembers. "There was no mutual interaction and no mutual cooperation. The trust was destroyed."

Emmanuel decided to reach out to friends they had in Nguruka to see if they could help: "Not all the people are Christian or Muslim. Others are neutral. I communicated with friends, with Muslims and Christians to see the possibility if we could sit together. They responded positively to the idea."

They worked hard to raise funds and identify people to come to a facilitated meeting. They were very clear: there had to be a balance of Muslims and Christians, and gender. Joel continues:

I remember it was very hard because some of the members who were supposed to attend did not attend... some of these people were reluctant... On the spot we decided to look for others... We told them there is a peace seminar. We want to restore peace, but we can't restore peace if you are not skilled enough, if you don't have the steps to [resolve] conflict. We want to train you so you can solve your own conflict.

[There was] one lady whose name was Amisa... Her husband was stopping her from attending the workshop... We went there and we had a meeting with the husband. We told him we are here to make sure that there is religious tolerance for both Christians and Muslims to worship freely without interfering with each other. And we are not here to preach Christianity or Islam. We are here to reconcile the two communities so that we can restore trust and mutual cooperation and live peacefully. The guy said, "I was wrongly understanding your way." After the talk he allowed Amisa to attend.

When we started the training, they didn't like to work together or sit together. What we have done, we started with a joke, light play... then Muslim and Christian prayers to show them that we are neutral... We told them to mix up and to sit in a circle. Also we told them they are free to contribute whatever they feel, to speak whatever they feel but make sure they respect both beliefs and respect human rights...

The meeting lasted for three days. Participants decided to set up a peace committee composed of Muslims and Christians, government officials, and key cultural leaders. That committee still functions, helping to resolve interfaith family and community conflicts.

*In everyone
There is a natural power
That can transform bad to good*

Joseph Mamai Makokha KENYA

Mamai is from Mount Elgon in Kenya. In 1997 his uncle was gunned down and killed, and everyone in his village had to flee, looking for a safe place. He was displaced from his home for two weeks before he could go back. In 2007, his nephew was taken away by a local militia and presumed killed, his body still unfound. When election violence erupted in Kenya in 2008, Mamai was chosen to serve as chairman of a newly formed group called the Friends Church Peace Teams. Mamai was among those to mediate between ethnic groups to help facilitate the peaceful return of the displaced back to their homes.

Some people had been driven out of their homes and their property was destroyed so they went into IDP [internally displaced people] camps. There remained those who had driven them away. And when the government directed that everybody go back to where they came from, particularly those who were in IDP camps, I wanted to know how prepared that group was, those that had been driven away. When we talked to them, they said they... feared [for] their lives because those who had driven them away were still there and nobody had talked to them. Therefore we initiated that idea of going to talk to those who had driven them away to see if they could accept them back... We talked to [them]... They at first resisted, they didn't want to hear anything to do with that group... In fact, at times, it looked like it was very dangerous to us because one thing they did not want to hear was those people to come back to their land. In one place we were almost stoned... They later on accepted that they could come back... Very interesting is that the exact people who had driven them away were the ones who received them and they went and slept with them in their houses. So it looked like it was a miracle because a real enemy now was accepting the one he had refused and he shared the same house with him.

There is that of God in everyone.
Even if our perceived enemies drove us away
I think there is something of God in that person.
I thought by reconciling with them
it is necessary for them also to change their heart
so that they see some good thing in me
like I have seen that good thing in them.

Let each see that of God in their perceived enemy.

Ndimurwamo Mathias BURUNDI

Mathias was one of only a few survivors at a gas station where mostly school children were herded and then burned. Later, he co-founded Burundi's first inter-ethnic peace committee that has helped weave the community back together. The peace committee has now become a model for similar initiatives throughout Burundi and the region.

I remember that day that I woke up and I was to go to my service, and when I crossed the road there were so many people in groups and they were talking. They had machetes and axes... It began to rain, and they put us inside the gas station... and others were searching for grass to use to burn us. There was a man who went to search for fuel to put on the grass so they could burn us. There were so many of us inside the gas station, there was no room to squeeze, and there was rope to tie us... Near the gas station there were pots of beer and those people took bottles and drank the beer and then threw the bottles on us and threw stones too. Inside the station, there was upheaval. After that, I got an idea. Inside the gas station, there was a stone and I took it and threw it through the glass of the window and got out through the window... I chose to die quickly instead of being tortured. At that time, I remember deciding to go out feet first, so that they may cut my legs first and my head after. I ran away and [was] treated at the hospital. My nephew, my uncle... [were] also in the gas station and died there. At that time I decided to set up a peace committee to thank God who protected me because I had nothing to give to God. I had to educate people morally, intellectually to tell them that to live in peace is something important. It took me a long time to change the mind of the victims of this event – I had to educate them even though it was difficult. I even had to punish small children because I would see them with stones and I would approach them to convince them to forget revenge.

When there is a conflict,
people must come together
and talk about the problem.
If you have done something bad to someone,
you need to approach them
and talk with them
and ask for forgiveness.
Because someone who is asked for forgiveness cannot refuse.

I think in this world there is no one who is holy.
We need to come together and find the answer.

Levy Munyemana DEMOCRATIC REPUBLIC OF CONGO

Levy works across ethnic groups in North Kivu, helping people in villages affected and displaced by ongoing armed conflict to seek ways to co-exist and develop joint strategies to mitigate violence and its consequences.

In 1993 I experienced ethnic violence. This was at 9am. I was going to the [town] centre. I was in a car with many people. We were going to a graduation ceremony. An ethnic group stopped our car. They said, you, get out. Because I was not of their tribe. They locked me in a small, small room. I waited just to die. I knew the person who wanted to kill me. He was a friend. I knew him very well. We [had] lived together. We [had] shared meals. I stayed in the small room for three hours. One person from the government army from Kinshasa was based there and he passed by the window and he saw me there. He asked me, "What are you doing here?" I said, "I am in prison." He said, "No, this is not a prison. They are going to kill you!" So he called the people. "Take this guy to prison, but not here." When they took me outside, a young man whom I [had] taught saw me. He took a bicycle to go home to tell the news. And some local authorities who were my close friends came to intervene and they accompanied me to my home.

Since I started these peacebuilding activities, I targeted these people who wanted to kill me. I invited them to the training. We discussed reconciliation. I shared my testimony during that workshop before those men. The impact that I saw was these people who were my enemies changed and became peacebuilders. So now I have these two people [who] are now working to build peace. I think that is an amazing impact.

Josephine Nyambikiye BURUNDI

Like most people in Burundi, Josephine was personally affected by the cycles of violence and long civil war in her country. Her brother, who had raised her, was killed in 1972. War erupted in 1993:

These things that happened in 1993 were revenge for what happened in 1972. So I was unhappy because I could see that these things would go on for a long time... When the rebels came in 1993, they came and found me in my house. They asked me for money and they beat me so very badly. I knew then my husband was not at home. [Afterward] he asked me to tell him the names of those people who did bad things like that. And I said, "No, I cannot tell you the names of those people because if I tell you the name of those people [and you take revenge] maybe they will come back and kill me and my whole family."

Josephine was invited to join a local peace committee composed of people who had fled their homes and were living in camps (mostly Tutsi), and Hutus from the neighbouring communities.

It was not easy to gather together. So the ones who were in the refugee camp said we cannot stay with them because we are not of the same ethnic group. And those who were in their home said, oh we cannot stay with those women [in the camp]... It was not easy, but using the word of God the things came better. Our friendship now started again... So when I was teaching them how to sew clothes, they saw that I was teaching both ethnic groups. And at that time we got a lot of meetings that were gathering us together and many women now started coming. And then we continued like that. So when the [Hutu] rebels came, the ones who remained in their home were the ones who came to the refugee camp and told those people, "Oh the rebels are coming, you have to run away." And when the [Tutsi] soldiers came, wanting to go to kill the people in their homes, those people [from the refugee camp] went and said, "You have to go because the Tutsi soldiers are coming to kill you."

To revenge is not good.
When you revenge,
you are the one who will have the conflict.
His children will come to revenge to your children too.

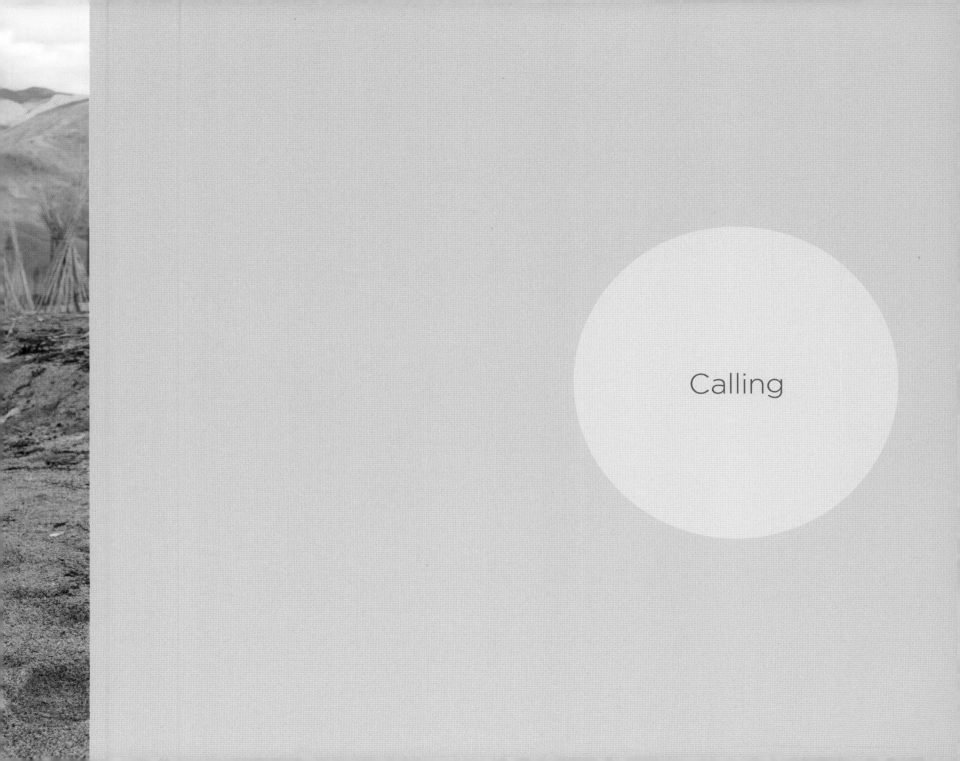

Calling

Benard Lismadi Agona KENYA

Agona is a community organiser, a pastor, a civic educator, and a nonviolent activist. He remembers, "I started suffering from pains in my chest and I could not understand what was happening, only to be told that they were caused by my bitterness, and I was developing some ulcers because of bitterness in my heart. That really made me to start thinking of alternative ways to start dealing with my problems." Today he is the field coordinator for a thriving and expanding active nonviolence programme in Kenya, the result of a partnership between Quaker Peace & Social Witness and Change Agents for Peace International. "I'm becoming a strong believer of nonviolence," he says, "because I believe it is the easiest way of attaining justice in life. All other means have failed."

I believe peace is not gotten from a silver plate.
You need to work for it.
You have to do something extraordinary.

Sometimes seeking for peace demands that you swallow your pride.
Sometimes it means that you let go your power.
The power in you,
the power to dominate
has to be let go.
The superiority complex in you has to be let go
so you remain flexible enough
so that you can be able to change your position.

I am a strong believer in possibilities.
Let us try nonviolence.
Let us try peace.
And see whether it will work.

Zawadi Nikuze DEMOCRATIC REPUBLIC OF CONGO

Zawadi Nikuze lives in North Kivu in Eastern DRC. The area has seen devastating levels of violence, widespread rape, and mass displacement of the population fleeing violence, and then dying of exposure, malnutrition and disease. Zawadi herself has been the victim of violence, including one incident when armed men invaded her home looking for money. As a peacebuilder, she accompanies rape victims in their journeys of recovery, and has been instrumental in bringing ethnic community leaders together for collaborative conflict analysis and grassroots peacebuilding.

The small gestures we do – maybe on our side we undermine them – but they mean a lot to someone who is oppressed. For instance, there is this case where after doing an individual listening session, I hugged this survivor as a way of thanking her for sharing her story with me. And as I was hugging her she just cried, and I wondered, "Have I done something wrong? Or did I do something wrong to interview her, just to listen to her?" But she said, "Zawadi, you know, I am impressed that you can hug me because no one wants to get close to me because of my situation."... So when I hugged her she was like, "Oh goodness such a person can hug me?'"And to me I just said, oh, I was just thinking that maybe these guys are in need of money or food, but even a hug can do magic. And to me that was like a turning point. Even a smile can change someone's life.

Give what you have.

If God has blessed you with a good smile
Give it to someone
who is stressed who needs it.

If God has given you the courage
of working with the vulnerable people
Go with them
Be near them…

Peace has no price.

Whatever you feel your heart is pushing you to do for peace
No matter how little it is
Do it
Because you just got today
We don't know what will happen tomorrow.

Discussion Guide

This book highlights people from one part of the globe, yet it tells a human story that belongs to us all. It is a story of the resilience and power of the human spirit. The people in these pages are ordinary people and their words of wisdom are universal. This guide suggests how we can interact with the stories in this book to reflect on our own lives and choices, no matter where we are and what we have experienced.

The stories can be used as a basis for small group discussions, personal reflection and journaling, or case studies in academic, workshop or conference settings. The content provides rich material to explore the themes of invisible and direct violence, trauma and trauma recovery, community level peacebuilding, and reconciliation.

Some of the questions included here may touch on difficult memories for people. The purpose of reflecting on these questions is to learn from the testimonies in this book and apply that learning to our own lives. However, sometimes it can be harmful to discuss past trauma if we are not equipped to deal with the strong emotions it can stir up in speakers and listeners alike. Some of these questions are more appropriate for personal reflection than group sharing. Those marked with an asterisk require a higher level of exposure and therefore risk.

If you use this book for discussion in a group, please bear in mind that you will need to prepare your group well in order for them to feel safe enough to discuss these challenging topics. You will need to discuss the issue of confidentiality and keep in mind the purpose of the conversation. Tread carefully with these discussions. The group needs to be prepared well and boundaries need to be established in order for participants not to feel an emotional overload. You might consider inviting to your discussion someone with experience of helping people process trauma. If you are concerned that someone in a group may have had a strong reaction, you should always ensure that they have been connected with a local counsellor.

Forms of Violence

1. The individuals in this book have all suffered violence, from the extremes of genocide or rape, to the structural violence of marginalisation and social exclusion, to the often hidden dynamics within family systems.
   a. Discuss the different forms of violence that are described through the stories.
   b. Are some forms of violence easier or more difficult to recover from?
   c. Is there any visible or invisible violence in your life? What is your relationship with that violence?*

Trauma and Recovery

2. Adrien Niyangabo says "Healing is different from fixing…. Healing asks courage, compassion, endurance, and also self-giving. It is risky also, so you need to understand that things will not unfold the way you are expecting."
   a. Why do you think Adrien suggests that healing is risky – what could someone risk by embarking on a journey of recovery?
   b. What does it mean to heal from an emotional trauma? Is it even possible?
   c. Is it necessary to heal from trauma or can it be managed? How have you coped with trauma in your own life?*

3. Cécile Nyirimana says, "Someone can't forgive with a broken heart." She says we need to "heal, then forgive, then love."
   a. What is your response to this quotation?
   b. What is forgiveness? Some think of forgiveness as a destination, a single act. Others think of it as an ongoing discipline.

c. Is forgiveness an essential ingredient of healing and reconciliation? Why or why not?

d. Think of your own experiences with forgiveness. Is there someone you have not forgiven? What are the consequences? What prevents forgiveness? What needs to happen to make it possible?*

Turning Points

4. Sizeli Marcellin says that in the midst of Rwanda's genocide he realised that although he was only one of four people in his family of 92 who had survived, there were others who had suffered more than him. This realisation was part of what pushed him to devote his life to helping others and to urge people to hold back from taking revenge.

   a. Think about difficult moments in your own life. Has it helped or hindered your own resilience to remember that there are others who have suffered more? Why?*

   b. Sizeli's story is one that is grounded in his Christian faith. How does your own spirituality or religious understanding play a role, if any, in the choices you make about conflict, revenge, and reconciliation?

5. Getry Agiza admits to having plotted to murder her stepbrother. While she may have been flirting with going to an extreme that most people never reach, her hurt and rage is something that has been experienced almost universally. She describes a poignant moment when she comes face-to-face with herself and makes a choice to take a different path.

   a. Have you ever experienced a level of hurt and rage that gives you insight into Getry's dilemma?*

   b. What inner and outer resources could you draw on to steer your choices in such a situation?

6. Abdul Kamara goes against his mother's wishes when he works with his former enemies in Sierra Leone. He says she "was very disappointed in me" and called him a "disgrace" for helping those who burned their house and raped his sister.

   a. Think about a time when you went against the wishes of those close to you. What was driving you? How did it make you feel?*

Taking Risks

7. Several of the stories give examples of people actively intervening between two groups in conflict or deliberately reaching out to the very people who tried to kill them.

   a. Do these small-scale interventions make a difference? Why or why not?

   b. "Whoever saves a life, it is considered as if he saved an entire world." How does this idea, found in both the Talmud and the Qur'an, relate to these stories?

8. Zawadi Nikuze urges us to "Give what you have." What are your gifts? What is your calling?

*Questions requiring higher level of exposure or risks

A brief history of Quaker peacework in Africa

Hezron Masitsa, Clerk

Quaker Peace Network – Africa

Although Quakers worldwide have worked tirelessly for peace for centuries, peacebuilding in Africa is still in its infancy. The subject of peacebuilding was taught in passing merely as one of the main values of Quakers.

In the 1990's Alternatives to Violence Project (AVP) was introduced to Africa, mainly South Africa, Kenya, Uganda, and Nigeria. The programme grew rapidly in South Africa as it offered an alternative response to injustices perpetrated by the apartheid regime. The Quaker Peace Centre in Cape Town arose out of a concern of the Cape Western Monthly Meeting of the Religious Society of Friends (Quakers) for the people affected by forced removals and apartheid. Initially the Meeting supported the work of a peaceworker until the work expanded and the Centre was formed in 1988. Quakers in Johannesburg also became involved in offering peace education. AVP expanded in Nigeria and Uganda during this period, though at a slow pace.

With the genocide in Rwanda and Burundi as the catalyst, international Quaker organisations such as the Norway sponsored Change Agents Peace Program (CAPP), American Friends Service Committee (AFSC) and Africa Great Lakes Initiative (AGLI), in collaboration with Friends World Committee for Consultation, Africa Section (FWCC-AS), intervened in the crisis that was slowly spreading to other African countries.
The efforts of several Quaker agencies contributed to strengthening African Quakers' capacity in peacebuilding to the extent that they have been able to grow their own institutions that are currently training and intervening in conflicts at different levels. Such institutions include Ministry for Peace and Reconciliation Under the Cross (Mi-PAREC) in Burundi, Friends Peace House in Rwanda and, in the Democratic Republic of Congo, the Friends Church (CEEACO) continues with peace activities through the CAPP programme. The events in the Great Lakes region provided Kenyan Quakers with lessons to learn from and they initiated AVP in 2003 as a conflict prevention mechanism. The 2007–8 post-election violence was such a challenge to Kenyan Quakers, leading to the creation of more structures for a coordinated approach to peacebuilding through the Friends Church Peace Teams (FCPT). Peacebuilding continues to multiply as a result of local grassroots initiated organisations.

African Quakers gather under the umbrella of Quaker Peace Network – Africa (QPN–Africa), an initiative begun in 1998 by three Quaker policy organisations (the Friends Committee on National Legislation (FCNL) in the USA, the Quaker United Nations Office (QUNO) and Quaker Peace & Social Witness (QPSW) in Britain). That first meeting, called the Quaker Consultation for the Peaceful Prevention of Violent Conflict, was held in England. The second meeting was held two years later, at QUNO New York and at the FCNL office in Washington DC. The next meeting was held in 2005 in Gitega, Burundi, at Mi-PAREC's Quaker retreat centre. It was at this conference that the idea of using a significant proportion of the time together for education was implemented, with presentations about 'Responding to Conflict', a method of analyzing peacebuilding activities. At this meeting it was also decided that the official name of the group would be Quaker Peace Network – Africa (QPN – Africa). QPN – Africa's main objective is to bring together peace practitioners from the Quaker network with a view to standing in solidarity with peace workers. In addition to the all-Africa gatherings every two or three years, QPN – Africa is now divided into four regions – QPN-East Africa, QPN-Central Africa, QPN-West Africa, and QPN-Southern Africa.

African Quakers' faith is founded on the Bible that shapes their core beliefs and practices. The Old Testament teaching that humankind is created in God's image has a profound influence on African Quakers' view of other humans and therefore the sanctity of human life. In addition, the New Testament presents Jesus' summary of the Ten Commandments as the Law of Love. The belief that God is love compels Christians to share this love of God with other human beings irrespective of their colour, race, sex, class, or any other form of peculiarity. These scriptures affirm the African philosophy of *Ubuntu* – *"I am because we are"*. A person is not an autonomous individual but a member of their society, family, clan, neighbourhood, or tribe. Quakers are therefore motivated to pursue social justice, equality, truth, peace, love, mercy, and forgiveness, with the understanding that these are important values that must be lived in accordance with the Kingdom of God.

About Quakers in Britain

The Quaker community circles the globe, spanning a rich diversity of regional cultures, beliefs and styles of worship. Most African Quakers follow Programmed or Evangelical traditions. Quakers in Britain share a way of life, not a set of beliefs. Their unity is based on a shared practice of silent worship (also described as unprogrammed), where they seek a communal stillness in which they wait for spiritual guidance leading to action.

Quakers try to live with honesty and integrity. This means seeking truth, including with people in positions of power.

The Quaker commitment to peace arises from the understanding that love is at the heart of existence and that all human beings are unique and equal. This leads Quakers to put their faith into action by working locally and globally to change the systems that cause violent conflict and injustice.

Acknowledgements

This book was made possible by the collective and largely voluntary efforts of many people in Africa and Britain. Quakers in Britain provided financial and spiritual support and without their commitment to the work this project would not have happened. Jacinta Makokha and Anne Bennett both separately planted seeds that eventually grew into the idea for this collection. Nigel Downes gave his time, his heart and his talent generously to the collection and production of the photographs. Elin Henrysson, Théoneste Bizimana and Benson Khamasi coordinated the interviews at the 2012 Quaker Peace Network – Africa gathering and in Burundi, Rwanda and Kenya. Frances Bowman in Britain contributed her empathetic insight and artistic talent to the realisation of the exhibition on which this book is based. The clerks and members of Quaker Peace Network – Africa actively supported the collection of material during their 2012 gathering and the last paragraph of the introduction is adapted from a keynote address they invited me to give at that meeting. Colleagues in Britain Yearly Meeting offered their time to read through drafts and give comments. Marigold Bentley, David Shipler and Hezron Masitsa all read the manuscript and offered valuable feedback. Matthew Chico shared a life with me in Rwanda, grounding me so that together we could "dwell deep". His support for this project, both emotional and practical, has been unwavering.

And over 40 peacebuilders in Africa offered their stories and their trust; they conducted many of the interviews with one another, listening and speaking with the hope that their words would touch hearts and make this world a better place. Some of those people are featured in this book.

Nigel Downes is an editorial and commercial photographer based in Qatar. He has worked around the world, including photographing street life in post-war Iraq and the aftermath of artillery fire on Palestinian refugees. He was official photographer for Qatar's successful 2022 FIFA World Cup bid and his work is regularly featured by major news outlets. He donated his time to participate in this project.

Laura Shipler Chico is programme manager for Peace-building in East Africa for Quaker Peace & Social Witness, a department of Quakers in Britain. She lived and worked alongside Rwandan Friends from 2005 to 2006 doing trauma recovery and reconciliation work in the wake of the genocide. She has been involved in peacebuilding, cross-cultural communication and social justice work in Asia, Africa and the USA. She currently lives in London with her husband and two sons.